Heidelberg City, Germany

Travel Guide, Tourism

Author
David Mills.

Publisher:
SONITTEC LTD
College House, 2nd
Floor
17 King Edwards
Road,
Ruislip
London
HA4 7AE.

Table of Content

Summary

The world is a book and those who do not travel read only one page.
It is indeed very unfortunate that some people feel traveling is a sheer waste of time, energy and money. Some also find traveling an extremely boring activity. Nevertheless, a good majority of people across the world prefer traveling, rather than staying inside the confined spaces of their homes. They love to explore new places, meet new people, and see things that they would not find in their homelands. It is this very popular attitude that has made tourism, one of the most profitable, commercial sectors in the world.

People travel for various reasons. Some travel for work, others for fun, and some for finding mental peace. Though every person may have his/her own reason to go on a journey, it is essential to note that traveling, in itself, has some inherent advantages. For one, for some days getting away from everyday routine is a pleasant change. It not only refreshes one's body, but also mind and soul. Traveling to a distant place and doing exciting things that are not thought of otherwise, can rejuvenate a person, who then returns home, ready to take on new and more difficult challenges in life and work. It makes a person forget his worries, problems, frustrations, and fears, albeit for some time. It gives him a chance to think wisely and constructively. Traveling also helps to heal; it can mend a broken heart.

For many people, traveling is a way to attain knowledge, and perhaps, a quest to find answers to their questions. For this, many people prefer to go to faraway and isolated places. For believers, it is a search for God and to gain higher knowledge; for others, it is a search for inner peace. They might or might not find what they are looking for, but such an experience certainly enriches their lives

Introduction

If any city in Germany encapsulates the spirit of the country, it is Heidelberg. Scores of poets and composers virtually the entire 19th-century German Romantic movement have sung its praises. Goethe and Mark Twain both fell in love here: the German writer with a beautiful young woman, the American author with the city itself. Sigmund Romberg set his operetta *The Student Prince* in the city; Carl Maria von Weber wrote his lushly Romantic opera *Der Freischütz* here. Composer Robert Schumann was a student at the university. The campaign these artists waged on behalf of the town has been astoundingly successful. Heidelberg's fame is out of all proportion to its size (population 140,000); more than 3½ million visitors crowd its streets every year.

Heidelberg was the political center of the Lower Palatinate. At the end of the Thirty Years' War (1618–48), the elector Carl Ludwig married his daughter to the brother of Louis XIV in the hope of bringing peace to the Rhineland. But when the elector's son died without an heir, Louis XIV used the marriage alliance as an excuse to claim Heidelberg, and in 1689 the town was sacked and laid to waste. Four years later he sacked the town again. From its ashes arose what you see today: a baroque town built on Gothic foundations, with narrow, twisting streets and alleyways.

Above all, Heidelberg is a university town, with students making up some 20% of its population.

And a youthful spirit is felt in the lively restaurants and pubs of the Altstadt (Old Town). In 1930 the university was expanded, and its buildings now dot the entire landscape of Heidelberg and neighboring suburbs. Modern Heidelberg changed as U.S. Army barracks and industrial development stretched into the suburbs, but the old heart of the city remains intact, exuding the spirit of romantic Germany.

History

Heidelberg's history dates back to the 5th century BC, when a group of Celts moved into the area. They built a fortress and church on the Heiligenberg, also known as 'Saint's Mountain'.

In 80 AD, the Romans arrived, setting up a permanent settlement on the bank of the Neckar River. A town grew up around the military camp and in the 8th century AD, historical records mention the village of Bergheim for the first time. Bergheim is today a district of modern Heidelberg.

From Medieval to Renaissance Times

Medieval Heidelberg history dates to the 12th century and the founding of a religious community here. In 1196, it is mentioned in records found in Schönau Abbey. The origins of Heidelberg Castle can be traced back to an early fortress on the site. In 1225, the castle came under the control of Louis I, the Duke of Bavaria. In 1303, another castle was built to defend the area and the ruins can still be seen today.

In 1386, Prince Elector Ruprecht I founded Heidelberg University. It was the third university to be founded within the Holy Roman Empire after Prague and Vienna, and today remains the oldest in Germany. It's thought that it owed its early success to an outbreak of plague in the nearby university city of Prague. Seeking an alternative place of education, many students opted for Heidelberg because it was considered far enough away from the source of contagion. In 1400, the

Heiliggeistkirche, or Church of the Holy Ghost, was built in the old market place. It was followed, in 1421, by the oldest public library in Germany.

In the mid-16th century, Prince Elector Otto Heinrich set about transforming the castle into a splendid building styled on Renaissance architecture. It is widely regarded as being one of the earliest German examples. Later, the castle was further extended, with the addition of its famous garden, gate and 'English Building'. Whilst the university managed to initially remain unaffected by the Reformation, it finally succumbed in 1556, when it was turned into a Protestant institution. In 1563, the university's Faculty of Theology contributed to the writing of the Heidelberg Catechism, essentially the textbook for the reformed faith in Germany.

Astle Attack and Peace Treaty

In 1622, Heidelberg Castle came under attack from General Tilly, a commander of the Holy Roman Emperor. That same year, the contents of the city's world-renowned library were confiscated and taken to the Vatican. Then, in 1688, French troops marched on Heidelberg and captured its castle. They left the following year, but not before they had destroyed its fortifications to prevent them being used in future attacks.

It wasn't until 1697 and the signing of a peace treaty that work on rebuilding Heidelberg could begin in earnest. This time, the new Baroque style of architecture was adopted. In the 18th century, Prince Elector Karl Theodor attempted to renovate the castle. However, in 1764, lightning struck the building, burning it to the ground and rendering it uninhabitable. Needless to say, after several further ill-fated attempts, he gave up

History from The 19th Century to Modern Times

The reorganisation of German states in 1803 was a turning point for the city's fortunes. The city was placed under the control of the Grand Duchy of Baden and its university became a state-owned institution. As a seat of learning, Heidelberg attracted many famous visitors. In 1880, the American author Mark Twain travelled here and, as a result, wrote 'A Tramp Abroad', a non-fiction travel book in which the city was to feature.

During World War Two, Heidelberg managed to survive with relatively little damage. This is largely because US forces took control of the city under General Patton and used it as their headquarters. Huge barracks were built in the southern part of the city at this time.

In the 1970s, work began on modernising the city, including the pedestrianisation of its main street.

In 1986, the Palatinate Library's contents were finally returned to Heidelberg as part of the 600th anniversary celebrations of the city's acclaimed university. It remains an important university city to this day and around a quarter of its population are students. It also has a large proportion of American residents.

Tourism

Heidelberg is beautiful

Heidelberg is considered one of the most beautiful cities in Germany. The picturesque ensemble of the castle, the Old Town, and the river Neckar surrounded by hills, which inspired the poets and artists of romanticism, still fascinates millions of visitors from all over the world today. But there's more to Heidelberg than romanticism.

Heidelberg is a city of science. It is home to Germany's oldest university, as well as to numerous others, and to a host of internationally renowned research institutes and research-based companies. The International Building Exhibition

(IBA) shows the city and the scientific community working together even more closely in the future.

Heidelberg is international. About 11.8 million visitors from all over the world come to the city each year. The population, too, is international: an estimated 45,000 of Heidelberg's inhabitants have an immigrant background – many of them are scientists and students.

Heidelberg is green. The combination of attractive countryside, favorable climate and urban lifestyle makes Heidelberg one of the leading cities in Germany in terms of leisure value. In addition, the city has received multiple awards for its commitment to the environment.

Heidelberg has a history. First mentioned in 1196, Heidelberg was planned and built, together with the castle, in the 13th century. Heidelberg's heyday as the capital of the Electoral Palatinate began not least with the foundation of the university – today the oldest in Germany – in 1386. Heidelberg was one of the few major German cities to be largely spared the destruction of the World War II.

Travel Guide

Get in

By plane

➢ Frankfurt (IATA: FRA) - The nearest intercontinental airport.

➢ Stuttgart (IATA: STR) - nice for European 'EU-domestic' flights.

ICE Train from Frankfurt or Stuttgart Airport to Heidelberg

You can travel to Heidelberg via ICE (Inter City Express), Germany's fastest train, running at 300km/h (180mph).

Both Frankfurt and Stuttgart airports have train stations inside the terminal. Frankfurt Airport even is a major ICE-train stop.

Reservations are not necessary; just buy your ticket at the counter or machine after you land. Credit cards are accepted; most staff speak English. It might be necessary to change trains (only once) at Mannheim, Stuttgart, or Frankfurt Central Station, but it is still likely to be faster than the bus. One way prices: Frankfurt €24.50 (ICE), Stuttgart €26 (IC) €38 (ICE).

Lufthansa Shuttle Bus
If you don't like trains, but prefer to see the German Autobahn, Lufthansa provides a shuttle bus from Frankfurt to Heidelberg for €23 one way and €42 round trip. If you have a Lufthansa Ticket, you get €2 discount.

Other Airports

Frankfurt-Hahn (IATA: HHN) - An airport in the middle of the beautiful green mountains of Hunsrück is a major hub for low-cost carrier Ryanair and also served by Wizzair. There are frequent bus connections from Heidelberg Hbf to Frankfurt-Hahn; the trip takes a little more than 2 hours, and ticket price starts from €5 if purchased in advance (as of 2016) .

Karlsruhe/Baden-Baden (IATA: FKB) - an airport served by Ryanair and a number of other low-cost carriers and charter flights. There are bus connections between the airport and Heidelberg Hbf; the trip takes less than 2 hours and the ticket price starts from €5 if purchased in advance (as of 2016) .

By train
The main train station Heidelberg Hbf is located in the western part of the city, from there you can

take a tram to any place downtown e.g. Bismarckplatz (taxis are not recommended as they are far more expensive than trams!) Check for connections to "Heidelberg Bismarckplatz" on German Railway Website

There are direct train lines from Heidelberg to Stuttgart, Karlsruhe, Mannheim and Frankfurt - and direct long distance trains to Munich, Vienna, Hamburg and Cologne usually running at least every 2 hours.

For most long distance destinations it is useful to take the regional train to nearby Mannheim Hbf (S-Bahn, about 15 minutes), from where there are frequent direct high-speed connections to all major cities in Germany and some places in the nearby countries (e.g. Paris, Zurich, Amsterdam).

Taking slow trains will be much cheaper on a Saturday or Sunday, especially if you have a five-person group ticket, "Schönes Wochenende", for €42 total or every day "Länderticket Baden-Württemberg" for € 22 - 38 total.

By car
The A5 connects Heidelberg directly to Frankfurt and Karlsruhe. It's easy to reach from any direction.

By bus
DeinBus.de is offering a bus to heidelberg from Frankfurt, Stuttgart, Cologne and many other cities. Tickets start at €9 one way and can be purchased directly from the driver.

Get around

The city runs a small but rather effective system of trams and buses. The two most important nodal points are the main station and *Bismarckplatz*. Bus #32 and #33 connect the main train station (Hauptbahnhof) with the old city area; detailed maps, schedules, and routes can be found online. A mountain railway runs between four stations (including the castle), linking the old city on the level of the river with the summit of the *Königstuhl* Mountain, about 400m (1312 feet) above the city.

Taxi service is available in Heidelberg. There is a taxi stand in the main train station. You can also hail a taxi in the street. Taxi fare in Heidelberg is 2.80 EUR flag fall plus 2.50 EUR per kilometer. The kilometer price decreases for long distance rides.

The "Heidelberg Card," a tourist pass that includes public transportation, many museums, and the lower section of the mountain railway (a separate fare is required for the upper section), can be bought at the tourist information center located just outside the main station.

Heidelberg's bike rental system works well. Up to four bikes may be rented from a Kiosk in central locations around the city. It cost two Euro for an hour. Bikes can be returned at any location throughout the city. Kiosks near busy transit hubs like the train or bus lines tend to rent out of bicycles more quickly than interior Kiosks located off the beaten path.

While tours and tour guides are available in German and English, you should plan ahead if you are visiting on a Sunday. English language guides are very hard to find them.

Seeing

Heilggeistkirche (Church of the Holy Spirit)

The Altstadt (historical city centre) and Hauptstraße (main street). The Hauptstrasse leads from Bismarckplatz across the old town. Approximately one mile in length, it is reputedly the longest pedestrian shopping street in Germany.

The Castle: an audio guide tour of the castle and its grounds is available for a fee near the entrance. It is available in several languages, including English. One can also take the guided tour that gives you access to the interiors of the castle not available otherwise. There is also a statue to the German poet Johann Wolfgang von Goethe in the castle gardens. Currently covered with unsightly scaffolding but this is very normal.

The Philosophenweg (walking path) which can be found on the northern side of the city. It provides a wonderful view across the oldest part of the city. Here you can find the site of the famous Merian Stich (engraving) which is a popular illustration of Heidelberg.

The Heiligenberg mountain which boasts a wonderful view over the old town.

The Thingstätte on top of Heiligenberg (an open-air theatre built by the Nazi regime in 1934 to host propaganda events)

Also on the Heiligenberg the remnants of a wall ancient Celts built to keep Germanic tribes out, the Heidenloch, a deep well with unknown origins, and the ruins of a 10th century cloister.

The Kurpfälzisches Museum on the Hauptstraße contains interesting exhibits of items from Heidelberg's pre-history to modern times.

The old university on Universitätsplatz in the old city and the adjacent old armory which is now a student cafeteria (but also open to the public).

Jesuitenkirche has 1712 Baroque construction with modern touches inside.

The Heiliggeistkirche church is only one of many large and small churches, but definitely the one with the most interesting history. During the dark ages, it was the shelter of the Bibliotheka Palatina, Germany's oldest library. The Bibliotheka was stolen and brought to Rome but eventually returned in pieces. Today, parts of it can be visited in the University Library (also the oldest and probably the most valuable of its kind in Germany), which is situated close to the old university.

You can get a great view of the Heiliggeistkirche, Old Town, and the Neckar river bridge from the castle (Schloss Heidelberg).

Doing

The city boasts more than eight theaters, including

➢ Stadttheater the large state-run theater, and

➢ Zimmertheater on Hauptstrasse, Germany's oldest private theatre

There are also many progressive culture hubs, including the famous Karlstorbahnhof in the east-end of the old city.

Königstuhl-Mountain, 568m (1560 ft) high, 450m (1480 ft) above Heidelberg, is a nice option to escape the hustle and bustle of Heidelberg downtown. The mountain top of Königstuhl offers a nice view over Heidelberg and the Rhine Valley. In good weather conditions you can see the Northern Black Forest. The same funicular railway that carries visitors to the castle continues to the mountain top. You will have to change trains once the final one to the top is a historical wooden funicular train. (A separate fare is required for the historical funicular.) On the top you can have a look at the more-than-100-year-old engine that just pulled you up. (No worries made in Germany!)

If you feel more energetic, you can take the Himmelsleiter (Heaven's Ladder or Sky Ladder) a stairway of 1200 steps winding up 270m (890 ft) up to Königstuhl. It ends 10m east of the mountain top funicular station. The lower end of stairs is just above the castle, but a bit hidden - ask locals or look it up on this map.

Buying

➢ Don't miss out the exquisitely stocked but quite expensive record shop Vinyl Only on the university square.

➢ For books in English, try The English Bookstore at Plöck 93 (tel: 06221-183001).

➢ Go by the Cathedral during the day for small markets selling souvenirs

Eating

BBQ & Beer - On sunny summer days the "Neckarwiese" ('Neckar meadow', northern bank of Neckar river, just west of Bismarckplatz) is full of people relaxing in the sun, having a Barbecue or a beer... This place also offers a nice view to the castle. You will have to bring your own grill, beer and steaks. Cheap grills to use once are availible at the "Bauhaus" do-it-youself store at Kurfürsten-Anlage 11, just 200m south of Bismarckplatz. Nice way to mix with locals.

Snacks: Along the Hauptstrasse, which runs through the centre of town, you will find several bakeries that serve local specialities including "Brezeln" (pretzels). Department stores have a nice selection of delicatessen stalls called "Markthallen" where you can eat everything on the spot.

Many of the cafes in Heidelberg set up outside tables when the weather is fair, and these are enjoyed by locals and tourists alike. A popular destination for summer cafe beer sipping and lounging is the Marktplatz, which is adjacent to the Heiliggeistkirche.

Meals: The Haupstrasse is plentiful with an amazing variety of restaurants. Dishes tend to be served in large portions, relatively inexpensive and of good quality. You can find something for almost every taste including Japanese, Indian, Italian, Chinese, German and Bavarian. American fast food and "Döner" restaurants cater to the budget conscious and late-night crowds.

Mensa im Marstallhof Maybe the most beautiful University Canteen in Germany, offering food and beer at low prices in a historic buildling and a Beer Garden!. Everybody is welcome, Open till late...

> Sunisas Thai Imbiss, Speyerer Straße 1, 69115 Heidelberg, 6221 / 6555533: if you want a change from German food: an

authentic, tasty Thai diner and takeaway with reasonable prices. It also has terrace, pool tables and cocktails. Open at 11am till late at night.

- Korean/Sushi restaurant, Heiliggeiststraße 3, close to the Marktplatz, next to the Hotel zum Rathaus, a seemingly little-known, but great sushi place (also serves Korean food).

- Zum Goldenen Anker, Rungenweg, 6221 / 4862

- Elia, Promenadeplatz, 6221 / 7820

- Turmstube, Schützenstr. , 6221 / 20114

- Kashmir, Strasse, 6221 / 20719

- Rizo, Lorchheimer-Str, 6221 / 8801

- Eatery, Breisacherstr. , 6221 / 10079

- Nabucco, Eichenweg, 6221 / 18191

- Perazza, Buschkoppel, 6221 / 7234

- Roter Ochs, Kumlbacher Str., 6221 / 6528

- ➢ Die Eselin, Aberlestraße , 6221 / 13489

- ➢ Bierhelder Hof, Schönfeldstrasse , 6221 / 811

- ➢ Kao Kao, Haupstr, 6221 / 14012

- ➢ Falafel, Heugasse . Serves lebanese cuisine with good vegetarian options.

- ➢ La Locanda 26, Steubenstrasse 26, +49 (6221) 7268922, . Opening Hours: 11.00 - 23.00 / Wednesday closed. middle.

- ➢ BrunnenStube (Restaurant BrunnenStube), Kranichweg 15, 6221 734222, . Mon.-Sat. from 17:00, closed Sundays and some public holidays;. Nice restaurant with modern German cuisine and moderate prices. Great fish, lamb and many seasonal specials. Located to the west of Heidelberg's centre in a living area. Patio dining in summer. Main course from 7.90 EUR to 18.90 EUR.

➢ Indian Palace (Indian Palace), Karlsruher Straße 74, 69126 Heidelberg, Germany.

➢ Vetter, Steingasse 9 69117 Heidelberg (06221165850).

Drinking

More than 300 bars, pubs, clubs, discotheques and the like, from Bavarian style tourist restaurants with deer antlers on the walls to extremely left-wing student bars which reserve the right to refuse police officers entry to the bar. You name it. Find your place and enjoy yourself. Heidelberg knows no curfew. Most bars close at 1am, but especially the students bars are often open until the early morning. Although the locals even the police officers are used to drunk tourists as well as to drunk students, please be calm on your way home and do not riot. As a remnant of the student revolts, Heidelberg has the largest ratio of policemen per capita and you may find yourself in the arms of an officer much faster than you think.

If you are a young person and happen to discover one of the student parties (which are quite numerous but advertised mostly by word-of-mouth), you scored the jackpot. Get inside, get a (dirt cheap) beer and have fun. But try and avoid being recognised as a tourist. No party ends before 3am and many run until 6 or 7am. Either Untere Straße or the Zieglers (Heidelbergs oldest students' bar) are frequently crowded with students.

Wines are produced around Heidelberg (e.g. Schriesheim, Wiesloch), but it might be difficult to get hold of them - unless you simply go to a vineyard... When you buy wine, always a safe bet is a Riesling from Pfalz or some white wine from Baden instead, or try any of the numerous wines from other German wine regions.

Vineyards Vineyards are usually located in the middle of small towns along Bergstraße (Highway B3). Fruit farmers sell wine right on their farm e.i. vineyard - make sure you also ask for Apple Wine (Hesse specialty) and New Wine (wine still in process of fermentation - sold from the barrel, bring a canister!) which you can sometimes drink in some 'wine-beergarden' right on site. Take a tram (5/5R) northbound to any place between Schriesheim and Lützelsachsen or a local train (S3/S4) southbound to Wiesloch - or (even better, if you have the time) S1 or S2 to Neustadt, where you will find yourself in an endless landscape of vine stocks.

Next to the Old Bridge, there are two small breweries: The Kulturbrauerei in the Leyergasse and Vetter's Brauhaus in the Steingasse. Vetter's is famous for having one of the strongest beers in world (Vetter 33).

➢ Mensa im Marstallhof Maybe the most beautiful University Canteen in Germany and maybe also Heidelberg's cheapest Beer Garden. Serving Welde-Beer (the Beer with screwed bottle necks and answering on any question...) Everybody is welcome, Open till late...

➢ If you want to mix with the locals, try the Untere Strasse, which runs between the Hauptstrasse and the river, parallel to both. It is packed with the student bars, including the crowded:

➢ Großer Mohr. Small but highly recommended. Tuesday night the odds are high to find the Mohr besieged by medical students. Thursdays are also Ladies Night, where girls receive free Sekt, making it a popular destination leading up to the weekend.

- ➢ Sonderbar. The latter boasts a huge collection of absinthe, whiskeys and whiskys, as well as a very distinctive atmosphere.
- ➢ Destille . There is a tree in in the center of the establishment.
- ➢ O'Reillys, . An Irish pub north of the river, just over the bridge from Bisi (Bismarckplatz).
- ➢ Dubliner A good Irish pub at the center of Heidelberg Mainstreet (Downtown)
- ➢ Ham Ham's A great place to chill, drink, and smoke.
- ➢ Nektar A very relaxed and chill place to enjoy a drink and party
- ➢ B.J.Z. Bar Great place to party in Emmertsgrund, its a B.Y.O.A. (Bring your own alcohol) and you can crash anywhere in the house

- ➢ The Brass Monkey Friendly bar on Haspelgasse, just opposite the old bridge. Good crowd and all staff also speak fluent English.
- ➢ Heidelberg Castle Cellar The cellar in the castle, where you get to see the Heidelberg Tun, also sells local Wines. Be sure to taste the Eiswein they have.

If you are looking for coffee rather than alcohol, Star Coffee has two branches, one off Bismarckplatz and the other on the Hauptstrasse, serving a variety of coffees and offering free WiFi access. Fewer computers but more style are found in the two Moro Cafes , directly at the Alte Brücke and one on the Hauptstraße.

Recently, most pubs close much earlier in the night, even on the weekends at around 2am. Just move to one of the numerous clubs, which usually have no entrance fee this late at night.

Be Safe

Heidelberg is an extremely safe city (even by German standards). However, women walking alone at night should take the usual precautions they would do anywhere else. Walking along the northern Neckar banks at night would not be advised, except in groups, particularly by the Studentenwohnheime (dorms). The shrubs are thick and it is very dark.

Usually there won't be any problem. If you are a bit 'paranoid' you can take a Taxi. If you are from New York, you might think they are cheap - if you are from East-Europe or Asia you will feel like they are ripping you off... use as needed. There are also "Frauentickets" available for women, you can buy these coupons for 8€ and they will cover the fare for anywhere in the city.

Don't walk on bicycle lanes! - Really don't! (they are often painted in red, but always separated from the pedestrian lanes by a white line): Heidelberg has more cyclists than motorists, and many of them have a rather cavalier way of riding. The southern parallel street to *Hauptstrasse* (called *Plöck*) is the main traffic channel for student cyclists between Bismarkplatz and University Square. During the day it can be such a buzz, it's already a sight worth visiting. But watch out: Many cyclists feel safe from the tourists there and lose all their good manners.

Sleeping

Budget

✓ Youth Hostel Heidelberg International

Jugendherberge Heidelberg International, Tiergartenstrasse 5, 69120 Heidelberg (″), +49 (0)6221 65119-0 (). checkin: 13:00; checkout: 10:00. Large, well maintained hostel, located next to the zoo on the eastern bank of the Neckar River, 25min walk away from the central rail station. Public transportation: take bus 32 from central rail station towards north (Sportzentrum Nord), get off at Jugendherberge stop. Dorms from €24.00 including breakfast and linen, various concession apply. Pre booking recommended. Towels can be rented from the reception for additional €2.

Steffi's Hostel Heidelberg, Alte Eppelheimer Str. 50 (Just walk straight out of the station and cross the big street and the tram rails in front of you. On the other side there's a modern building, where you enter a shopping arcade (Kurfürstenpassage – Jack Wolfskin / Backpacker Store). Again you walk straight ahead through the passage and leave it on the opposite side. From the exit you can already see a big brick stone building in front of you. Here on the third floor above the Lidl supermarket, Steffis Hostel Heidelberg is situated.), +49

(0)6221/7782772 (), . checkin: 10am - 1pm and 5pm - 8pm; checkout: until 12. Dorms from €20, everything included.

Hotel ISG, . *Hotel ISG* is located in the suburb of Boxberg is about a 15 minute taxi ride from central Heidelberg. Fitted out in the Bauhaus style the rooms are comfortable enough (and the bathrooms are excellent) but there is nothing to do in Boxberg.If you are visiting the EMBL, however, it is very convenient, as a free shuttle runs from the hotel to the institute.

Hotel Restaurant Scheid. Hotel Restaurant Scheid is a nice, quiet, reasonably priced hotel in the suburb of Schriesheim, a short tram ride north of Heidelberg.Schriesheim is built on a hill so if you are hitting the clubs, don't forget about the late 30 min. night walk up the hill from the tram stop

(Schriesheim Bahnhof) to Hotel Scheid. Phone +49 (0)6203 6050.

Mid-range

The Ritter, Hauptstraße 178, (), . The Ritter is the oldest building (1592) in Heidelberg that has outlasted all fires and wars that have haunted the city over the times. It can get a little noisy considering its location directly at the heart of the Altstadt. Also a picturesque photo opportunity.

Hip Hotel, Hauptstrasse 115, . This was revamped in 2005 as a boutique hotel. Each room is modeled after a famous city, the most interesting room being the Zermatt (for Heidi and skiing fans).

Hotel Neu Heidelberg, . *Hotel Neu Heidelberg* is located in the west of Heidelberg's center. Recommendable 3 star hotel with lovely restaurant, nice breakfast buffet, terrace, garden, wlan, bicycles for guests, free parking, various int.

tv channels, etc. Easily reachable by car and public transportation.

<u>NH Hotel Heidelberg</u>, . Located about 1km west of the edge of the Altstadt, situated in an old brewery. However its been totally renovated and fitted out in a modernist decor, all glass, wood floors and exposed metal. Some of the rooms are very pleasant, though the ones overlooking the main road can be noisy. Food in the bar is disappointing.

<u>Crowne Plaza</u>, . A fairly standard anonymous business hotel is located just off Bismarckplatz. Rooms near the lifts can be extremely noisy, so are best avoided

<u>Holiday Inn Heidelberg</u>, Pliekartsfoerster Strasse 101, (toll free: 0800 181 6068), . checkin: 15:00; checkout: 11:00. Standard hotel that's about 5km outside of the centre of Heidelberg. Amenities

include a sauna and gym. Internet access comes at a hefty minimum price of €10 for 60 minutes or €17 for 24 hours if travellers are only looking to browse. For business users, it's even more expensive. €198 +.

Hotel Holländer Hof Heidelberg , Neckarstaden 66, Tel: +49 6221 60500. The hotel has a unique view of the Neckar River and the Philosopher´s Walk. It is located in the middle of the historical old city centre, just opposite the Old Bridge. The famous Heidelberg castle, as well as all sights of Heidelberg can be reached within a few walking minutes. The Restaurants and the pedestrian area are located around the corner.

Splurge
Der Europäischer Hof, . Located just on the edge of the Altstadt *Der Europäischer Hof* a classic privately owned five star hotel. Pleasant

atmosphere and attentive staff. Most of the rooms look out over the courtyard and are therefore admirably quiet. Since 1865 der EUROPÄISCHE HOF has been a home from home for cultivated travelers in search of timeless traditional charm, atmosphere, and service. The name of the establishment stands for all that is best in European hotel culture and for exceptional standards of service. Official listings have rated the hotel as the finest hotel in Heidelberg and in the Rhine-Neckar Metropolitan Region. The hotel is a Certified Business Hotel, Certified Conference Hotel, and certified as conforming to the pharma code. Accordingly, they have everything you expect of a professional business hotel.

Hirschgasse Heidelberg, Hirschgasse 3 - 69120 Heidelberg, +49 6221 4540, . checkin: 3 PM; checkout: 12 AM. The *Hirschgasse* is the oldest Hotel of Heidelberg and the oldest student dwelling house of Germany. It was first mentioned in a love story in 1472 and is nestled in a little side valley of a select residential area opposite the Heidelberg castle. An impressive walk along the River Neckar will take you to the Altstadt on the other side of the river. Mark Twain wrote about this in his book "A Tramp Abroad." The rooms are all unique and will delight Laura Ashley fans and the ones seeking a good shot of authentic romantic ambiance. It comes along with two restaurants: the historic Mensurstube with regional dishes and over 250 year old tables, even Count Otto von Bismarck carved his name into. The elegant Le Gourmet is a classic French restaurant with attentive but yet uncomplicated service and will delight your credit cards with a good value for a swipe. A vineyard only a stone's throw away from the hotel "Sunnyside upon the

Bridge" provides a good local Riesling or Late Burgundy. from 125 to 335.

Tourist Attractions and Sightseeing

Heidelberg is a pedestrian-friendly city--especially in the Altstadt, or Old Town, where your explorations are likely to begin.

The Altstadt is a long, narrow strip of medieval cityscape on the south bank of the Neckar River. Most sights are within a block or two of the Hauptstrasse or Main Street, which runs--with an occasional name change--from the department stores of the Bismarkplatz to the Karlstor at the eastern end of town.

Major sights in the Altstadt are well-documented in a German-language guidebook, *Marco Polo: Heidelberg*, which also covers such topics as hotels, dining, shopping, and nightspots. Even better, if you don't read German, is the English-language *Castle and City Guide Heidelberg am Neckar* (which isn't as comprehensive or up to date as the Marco Polo guide and may be hard to find). For other guidebook titles, see your bookseller or Amazon.com.

Our advice: Get hold of a map (such as the 1:15000 *ADAC CityPlan*, shown at left), or use the map in your guidebook to explore the Altstadt as the spirit moves you.

Visit the Alte Universität with its historic assembly hall; a combined ticket will also get you into theStudentenkarzer, where academic miscreants did time for drunkenness, womanizing, pig-stealing, and other sins from the 1500s until 1914

Wander into the churches, especially the Gothic Heiliggeistkirche on the Marktplatz (with its built-in market stalls) the Jesuitkirche, and the

Peterskirche (Heidelberg's second-oldest church, dating back to 1316).

Walk down the Steingasse toward the river, where you'll encounter the Brückentor (Bridge Gate) and the Alte Brücke or old stone pedestrian bridge across the Neckar, which inspired Goethe to gush about its beauty when he first saw it in 1797. Walk out onto the bridge and enjoy the views of Heidelberg's river, old town, and castle.

Schloss Heidelberg, deserves a full morning or afternoon: It's on a hill behind the Altstadt, which you can reach on foot (via winding streets or paths) or with the Heidelberger Bergbahn , which runs to the castle and on up to theKönigstuhl with its long-distance views, falconry center, children's fairy-tale park, and other attractions.

The Schloss is a pleasant combination of ruins, restored rooms (complete with guided tour), a massive wine vat, viewing terraces, an excellent pharmacy museum , and even a wedding chapel that attracts vast numbers of Japanese couples. You can walk along the outside of the castle free of charge; to go inside, buy a ticket at the office near the funicular station, and book a sightseeing tour once you're inside the grounds.

Local tours

Heidelberg's tourist office has inexpensive guided walking tours year-round, with English narration available several days of the week from spring through fall. German-language evening tours and bilingual bus tours are also available.

If you understand German, you might enjoy an historic walking tour with Stadtfuehrungen Heidelberg, which offers such themed tours as "Henker, Hexen, Huebschlerinnen" (led by the "executioner's daughter") and "Werwölfe, Wiedergänger und Vampyre."

Full of enjoyable tourist attractions, visitors will fall in love with Heidelberg's charming medieval architecture and river setting. The atmospheric Old Town offers endless narrow streets, historic attractions and a handful of stunning churches, all overshadowed by the imposing Heidelberg Castle.

For the most scenic views of the Heidelberg cityscape, head for Philosophenweg, a short hike from the city, or alternatively, sit comfortably and enjoy the scenery at a steep angle on the Bergbahn (mountain railway). The city's dominant tourist attractions are below.

Bergbahn

Address: Bremeneckgasse / Burgweg, Parkhaus P12, Heidelberg, D-69117, Germany, DE

Tel: +49 06211 513 2150

Heidelberg's 100-year-old mountain railway (Bergbahn) is one of the city's most popular tourist attractions, with the lower railway taking visitors from the Kornmarkt to Castle Station, then onwards to Molenkur Station. From here, the upper railway begins, travelling to Koenigstuhl, which is around 560 metres / 1,837 feet high. The slow climb on both railways provides scenic views out over the city.

Open hours: daily - 09:00 to 20:30, seasonal variations apply

Admission: charge

Neckar River Cruise (Rhein-Neckar Fahrgastschifffahrt)

Passenger boats leave from the Old Town for cruises along the Neckar River. Typically lasting around two or three hours, you can relax and enjoy the lovely views of the valley as you gently float past centuries-old villages, towns and their many attractions. The running commentary means you can learn about the sights en-route. Depending on the weather, you can choose from open-top or covered boats.

Open hours: daily, seasonal variations

Admission: charge, discount for children

Neuenheim Market

Address: Neuenheim Market, Heidelberg, Germany, DE

If you want a taste of 'real' German life, Neuenheim Market offers a typical Heidelberg shopping experience with an old town feel. The twice-weekly market sells mainly fresh produce, including locally made cheeses, colourful flowers and deliciously fresh vegetables. The Mercedes, Porsche and BMWs that tend to pull up here reveal the market may not be the most inexpensive in the region, but at least you know what you're getting is good quality.

Open hours: Saturdays and Wednesdays - 07:00 to 13:00

Admission: no charge

Walking Tours / Old Town (Altstadt)

The old town is the heart and the historical center of Heidelberg . First documented in 1196, it is world famous for its unique triad of city, mountains and river . The medieval city layout with narrow streets and baroque old buildings, the upper-class hillside development on the Königstuhl, and the castle towering over the old town as well as the monuments and sightsattract around three million visitors each year .

The old town covers approximately 1,380 hectares, of which only 9.8 percent are cultivated . The district is characterized by the forest area of the Königstuhl , which, at 564 meters, is one of the highest mountains in the Odenwald.

At the same time, the old town is also home to around 10,000 Heidelberg residents . Like the visitors, they appreciate the short distances , the multitude of cultural and leisure facilities, the attractive shopping facilities with over 400 shops and the extensive gastronomy and hotel offerings . Since November 2012, the Heidelberg Theater in the Old Town has also been reopened: A nationwide unique commitment of the city and private donors has made the renovation and expansion of the theater possible.

The historic center of Heidelberg is the founding seat of the oldest university in Germany (founded in 1386), the "Ruperto Carola", and is home to many internationally renowned institutions of the university. Students from all over the world visit the Heidelberg University, buffle in one of the most magnificent university libraries and give the old town a youthful, international flair.

Address: Altstadt, Heidelberg, Germany, DE

A walking tour of Heidelberg's primary district is a must, with it possible to cover most of the main attractions on foot in just a few hours. Wander through the narrow cobblestone streets starting at Bismarckplatz and make your way to the pedestrianised Hauptstrasse, the main tourist shopping area in Heidelberg. Visit the old Baroque-style university, the former students' prison at Jesuit's Church (Jesuitenkiche) and Castle Markplatz for excellent views. If your feet are weary, stop for a coffee here in the shadow of the Gothic Holy Ghost Church (Heiliggeistkirche). Nearby attractions include Knight's House (Haus zum Ritter), the oldest private house in the whole of Heidelberg, dating from 1592. At the river you can admire the Bridge Gate (Brukentor), which leads to the Renaissance style Old Bridge (Alte Brucke). Don't forget to have your photo taken with the Heidelberg monkey.

Open hours: daily - 24 hours

Admission: no charge

The Castle of Heidelberg

The ruins of the once grand *Schloss Heidelberg* (Heidelberg Castle) rise up on a rocky hilltop over the university town of Heidelberg. While young students and busloads of visitors trundle about below, Heidelberg Castle presides above, drawing an estimated 1 million visitors a year.

History

Once a Gothic masterpiece, the Castle of Heidelberg has encountered turbulent times. The earliest structure was constructed in the early

1300s and continued to grow and expand until it became two castles by 1294.

Dark times were ahead, however.

It was plundered and burned by the French army in 1689, then struck by lightning 100 years later. Lightning struck twice as another bolt in 1764 destroyed what little had been rebuilt. The ruins were further plundered to use the red brick to build new houses in the town.

Unlike many German castles, the Castle of Heidelberg never regained its original glory and still lies in partial ruins. But the ruins have a ragged charm of their own. Each building highlights a different period of German architecture and the ruins are considered the symbol of German Romanticism and the Castle of Heidelberg is one of the highlights of the German Castle Road.

Attractions

Visitors start their trip by admiring the castle from afar. It dominates the skyline, presiding regally above the turbulence of daily life. Once you have reached the castle grounds, stop and look back at the city and iconic bridge.

It is quite the view as visitors roam the elegant castle gardens for free.

For the full experience, buy an entrance ticket to the castle to explore the spectacular interiors. A guided tour will help you appreciate the many stories this castle holds. For example, the Ottheinrich Building is one of the earliest palace buildings of the German Renaissance.

Adorned with impressive sculptures, *Herrensaal* (Knights' Hall) and the Imperial Hall house many of the special exhibitions. Or that *Fassbau* (wine cellar) from 1590 which houses the biggest wine barrel in the world, Heidelberg Tun, which holds

220,000 liters (58,124 gallons) of wine. Or stand in front of the Friedrich Building and gaze up at the emperors and kings from the palace courtyard. Or the story about Mark Twain who visited the castle back in his day, and the subsequent boat trip on the nearby Neckar river that allegedly inspired him to write a chapter of *Huckleberry Finn*.

Three times every summer, *Schlossbeleuchtung* (castle lighting) and fireworks take place. This is to commemorate when the castle burned (1689, 1693 and 1764).

After climbing to the top, you might be in need of sustenance. While the ancient kitchens may not be up to feeding the masses, the Heidelberger Schloss Restaurants includes an elegant *Weinstube*, bakery, and special events space.

How to Get There

Heidelberg Castle is located at Schloss Heidelberg, 69117 Heidelberg, Germany, 57 miles south of Frankfurt. Here's how to get there:

- ✓ By car: Take the Autobahn (motorway) A 5 or A6 into the direction of Heidelberg; exit onto the Autobahn A 656, which will take you into the center of Heidelberg

- ✓ By train: Take the train to Mannheim and then hop on a regional train to Heidelberg, which is only 15 minutes away

Once you reach the foot of the castle hill, visitors can climb it by foot, or take a historic cable car up to the castle. This 1.5km ride is the longest cable car route in Germany reaching a height of 550 meters up past the castle to Königstuhl.

Heidelberg Student Prison

The University of Heidelberg has a long tradition as a center of learning, but students at the 500-year-old uni have often taken the view that "All work and no play makes Hans a dull boy." As long ago as the 16th Century, citizen complaints about carousing students led the university to open a Studentenkarzer, or Student Prison, where academic miscreants were kept off the streets for three days to four weeks at a time.

Over the centuries, the University of Heidelberg's Student Prison was moved several times, and it finally closed down in 1914. Today, that prison--with its original fixtures and graffiti--offers a glimpse into student life at the University of Heidelberg before World War I.

You enter the Studentenkarzer on Augustinergasse, around the corner from the Alte Universität, which was begun in 1712 and houses the University Museum. As you head the rickety stairs, you'll see student prisoners' graffiti everywhere: on walls, above the doors, and even on the ceiling. (For some fine examples, see page 2 of this article.)

The prison is about the size of a large apartment, with a door (now locked) that once allowed student prisoners to enter the Old University for classes during their confinement.

Being jailed in the Studentenkarzer couldn't have been too unpleasant, because time behind bars was a rite of passage for many students. The Heidelberg Tourist Office describes "the much-coveted stay in the 'Student Prison' for Town vs. Gown offenses, such as disturbing the peace, womanising, unruly drunkenness, and setting the townspeople's ubiquitous pigs free."

Museums

The rich historical, cultural and artistic heritage of the city is well-preserved within Heidelberg's many museums, which cover a whole host of interests. Those with a passion for textiles will be at home in the late Max Berk's Textile Museum, while the University Museum (Universitätsmuseum) is of special local interest, celebrating Heidelberg's famous and historic university campus.

If you are lucky enough to visit Heidelberg during the month of March, the 'Long Night of the Museums' is worth looking out for, where the city's many museums and similar venues stay open all night long, until as late as 03:00 in the morning, hosting live events and celebrations.

German Pharmaceutical Museum (Deutsches Apothekenmuseum)

Address: Schloss, Heidelberg, D-69177, Germany, DE

Tel: +49 06221 2 5880

Celebrating the history of alchemy and chemistry, the German Pharmaceutical Museum is part of Heidelberg Castle (Schloss) and is full of scientific memorabilia. Particularly noteworthy is the Robert Bunsen memorial, which remembers the life and works of the man who invented the much-used Bunsen burner, while other exhibits include various drugs and herbs, a laboratory, and many original pharmaceutical artefacts, dating back as far as the 17th century.

Open hours: daily - 10:00 to 17:30

Admission: charge, concessions available

Textile Museum (Textilmuseum Max Berk)

Address: Brahmsstrasse 8, Heidelberg, Germany, DE

Tel: +49 06221 80 0317

The city of Heidelberg has a long history of textile production, with textile producer Max Berk being responsible for the establishment of this privately funded museum in 1978. Housed in what was formerly a church, the Textile Museum is divided into various sections, displaying items such as clothing items and accessories from around the world. Detailing production methods, and the machinery and fibres used in the making of the textiles on display, adds an educational aspect to this interesting museum.

Open hours: Wednesday, Saturday and Sunday - 13:00 to 18:00

Admission: charge

University Museum (Universitätsmuseum)

Address: Grabengasse 1, Alte Universität, Heidelberg, D-69117, Germany, DE

Part of the university complex, the city's interesting University Museum pays tribute to the history of Germany's oldest university, the Ruprecht Karl University of Heidelberg, which was established more than 600 years ago. The museum features three main themed rooms, where visitors can learn more about this impressive educational institution.

Open hours: Tuesday to Friday - 10:00 to 18:00

Admission: no charge

German Packing Museum (Deutsches Verpackungsmuseum)

Address: Hauptstrasse 22, Heidelberg, D-69117, Germany, DE

Tel: +49 06221 2 1361

An unusual museum where the development of packaging and design is documented, the German Packing Museum is easy to find and stands in the heart of Heidelberg city centre. Housed within a former church building, the museum also features displays relating to city life through the years, with many exhibits of local significance.

Open hours: Wednesday to Friday - 13:00 to 18:00, Saturday and Sunday - 11:00 to 18:00

Admission: charge

Art Galleries

Art lovers will not want to miss the museums and art galleries within Heidelberg. Always popular is the city's Museum of the Palatinate, where you will discover the Frankenthal porcelain collection and many paintings from the Romantic period. If you want to break free from traditional museum settings, try appreciating art works while you get to grips with Heidelberg's exciting nightlife at the Halle 02.

For some of the best regional paintings, pay a visit to the Heidelberg Art Gallery, known locally as the Heidelberger Kunstverein. Information about the main art galleries is shown below.

Halle 02

Address: Güteramtsstrasse 2, Heidelberg, D-69115, Germany, DE

Tel: +49 06221 338 9990

Not a gallery as such, Halle 02 is a unique nightclub and mixes DJs with visual and performance arts. Enjoy everything from video installations to graffiti and photography, as you swing your hips to the beat. Open daily until the early hours, you will have to stay up late it you want to fully appreciate this set up, which won the Innovation Prize

(Innovationspreis) for best club in the state.

Open hours: daily - 21:30 until late

Admission: charge

Heidelberg Art Gallery (Heidelberger Kunstverein)

Address: Hauptstrasse 97, Heidelberg, D-69117, Germany, DE

Tel: +49 06221 18 4062

This art club and museum hosts frequently rotating exhibitions throughout the year, focusing on modern art works. Both international and national art is showcased at the Heidelberg Art Gallery, and guided tours are available two days a week. Also on-site is a library containing material on contemporary art. Keeping things lively are the multitude of art performances of all genres, including dance, music and drama, which are held in the exhibition hall year-round.

Open hours: Tuesday to Sunday - 11:00 to 17:00;

Wednesday - 11:00 to 20:00

Admission: charge

Museum Of Ancient Art (Antikenmuseum Und Abgusssammlung)

Address: Marstallhof 4, Neues Kollegiengebäude,

Heidelberg, D-69117, Germany, DE

Tel: +49 06221 54 2512

This impressive archaeological collection ranks as the largest university collection of its kind in Germany. Housed in the Marstallhof, visitors to the Heidelberg Museum of Ancient Art can appreciate ancient art works from the 4th century up until late antiquity. Not only displaying German finds, there are pieces from across the globe, including works from Mediterranean countries. The cast gallery is a highlight, displaying intriguing casts of famous Greek and Roman statues, made from plaster.

Open hours: Wednesday - 15:00 to 17:00 (cast gallery) and 17:00 to 19:00 (ancient art museum); Sunday - 11:00 to 13:00 (both collections)

Admission: no charge

Museum of The Palatinate (Kurpfälzisches Museum Im Palais Morass)

Address: Hauptstrasse 97, Heidelberg, Germany, DE

Tel: +49 06221 58 34 020

Presenting art and cultural history of the region, this fascinating collection is on display at the Baroque Palais Morass, worth visiting in its own right. The collection of portraits of the Prince Electors is a highlight, as are the extensive collections of Frankenthal porcelain, costumes throughout the ages and German coins. The gallery of sculptures and paintings at the Museum of the Palatinate houses works from the 15th through 10th century, showcasing pieces by Heidelberg's Romantics.

Open hours: Tuesday to Sunday - 10:00 to 18:00

Admission: charge, discount for students and on Sundays

Attractions Nearby Heidelberg

Many attractions are located close to Heidelberg and make for ideal day trips and excursions. Close to Heidelberg are various walking trails around its surrounding countryside, along the River Neckar and throughout the Neckar Valley, which is home to no less than four castles.

For wine lovers in Heidelberg, there is a wealth of vineyards and wineries nearby, offering wine tasting and tours, with the official German Wine

Route being a good starting point. The main attractions outside of the city are listed below.

Frankfurt Am Main

Around 88 km / 55 miles north of Heidelberg, the city of Frankfurt is a true city of culture. With a population of around 650,000 people and sited along the Main River, Frankfurt is known for its important financial centres, which include the city's important Stock Exchange and also the headquarters of the European Central Bank. Those looking to visit Frankfurt's main tourist attractions should consider a trip to the 14th-century Gothic-style Saint Bartholomeus' Cathedral, the Römer Town Hall, the Opera House, and the Museum for Modern Art. Frankfurt's historic old town area is particularly unusual, since it contains a mixture of historic and modern architecture, including many eye-catching skyscrapers.

Mainz

Mainz can be found approximately 93 km / 58 miles north-west of Heidelberg and is the state capital. The historic Altstadt quarter offers a collection of historic buildings and is close to the Rhine River, where you will find a number of appealing riverside trails, pathways and other attractions. Around the very centre of Mainz, the shopping streets, the 10th-century cathedral and Gutenberg Museum are all worthy of your attention.

Mannheim

Lying on the western outskirts of Heidelberg, Mannheim is a mere 21 km / 13 miles away from Heidelberg and was officially founded more than 400 years ago. Whilst not one of Germany's most popular cities, Mannheim does boast a big-city vibe, many fun attractions and plenty of things to see and do, a good shopping district, a fine selection of restaurants around the Planken area, the stunning Luisenpark, the 18th-century Baroque-style Mannheim Palace, and a comprehensive bus and tram network.

Stuttgart

Perhaps best known for being the official home of the famous German car manufacturers, Mercedes-Benz, Stuttgart and its many attractions can be reached in less than two hours and stands 128 km / 80 miles south-east of Heidelberg. Surrounded by a particularly important green belt and full of tourist appeal, when in Stuttgart, look out for its locally produced wine, historic zoological and botanical gardens of Wilhelma, and the nearby early 18th-century Ludwigsburg Palace and its eye-catching Baroque-style architecture.

Speyer

A historic town founded around 2,000 years ago, Speyer lies just 45 km / 28 miles south-west of Heidelberg and is home to just over 50,000 inhabitants. Lying alongside the Rhine River, central Speyer is fairly compact and the majority of the main attractions are within easy walking distance of each other, including the magnificent 11th-century Speyer Cathedral with its vaulted interior, and also tall city gate, which is the highest of its kind in Germany and known locally as the 'Altpörtel'.

Darmstadt

An important city sited on the southerly side of the Rhine Main Metropolitan Area, roughly 59 km / 37 miles north of Heidelberg, Darmstadt has a population of just over 140,000 people. Many of the main attractions in Darmstadt are centred around the Hauptbahnhof and Europaplatz area, and also the Old Town (Altstadt) area. The Palace of Darmstadt dominates much of the city centre, while the city's 13th-century Frankenstein Castle, the namesake of Mary Shelley's famous novel, enjoys an elevated setting and overlooks the city itself.

Top Tourist Attractions in Heidelberg

Heidelberg is an ideal destination for any traveler who wishes to experience the scenic beauty of the lush woodlands, old-town architecture and ruined castles of Germany's Rhineland. The city's picturesque location on the Neckar River in southwest Germany has made Heidelberg a top destination for tourists since the 1800s.

Praised by poets like Goethe, painted by artists like Turner and rhapsodized by composers like Schumann, Heidelberg embodies the spirit of the romantic Rhineland. As the country's oldest university town, it's a surprisingly lively city too, boasting an enticing array of pubs and restaurants that cater to the student population. With all the tourist attractions in Heidelberg, it's no wonder that so many consider this Germany city an essential stop on any European tour.

Kornmarkt

A bustling grain market in the Middle Ages, the Kornmarkt square was later home to a hospital run by Catholics in the 16th century. The layout of the hospital's chapel can still be identified by the paving in the square. In the 17th century, a statue known as Madonna at the Grain Market was erected as part of a Jesuit campaign designed to promote Catholicism. Today, the Madonna is regarded as a fine work of art that provides the perfect centerpiece to this pleasant town square. Visitors gather here to eat at open-air cafés and enjoy views of the Heidelberg Castle on the slopes above the Kornmarkt.

Heiligenberg

Also known as All Saints' Mountain, Heiligenberg rises above the city on the north shore of the Neckar River. Offering great views of both the river and the plains of the Rhine Valley, the mountain has long been valued for its defensive position. Artifacts have been excavated dating back to the Neolithic Era. Visitors can explore remnants of medieval monasteries, an ancient Roman temple and a Celtic fort built in the 4th century, B.C. The open-air theater known as the Thingstätte built during the Third Reich is on view as well.

Heiliggeistkirche

Located in the city's Market Square, the Heiliggeistkirche, or Church of the Holy Spirit, is Heidelberg's most famous place of worship. The original construction of the Gothic church began in

1398, but it wasn't completed until 1544. The church's Baroque steeple was added after a fire in 1709. Visitors can climb the 208 steps to the top of the spire for city views. The Heiliggeistkirche is unique in that has been used by both Catholics and Protestants at the same time. A partition wall separating the two congregations stood in place for more than 200 years.

Königstuhl

Heidelberg's famous castle is situated on the slopes of Königstuhl (Kings Seat Mountain), the second-highest peak in Germany's low Odenwald mountain range. An historic wooden funicular train takes visitors to the top for breathtaking views of the Neckar river valley and of the Black Forest beyond. There's a restaurant and kid's play area at the summit as well as a tight network of hiking trails. The clear air makes Kings Seat Mountain a great location for viewing the stars too. The

Heidelberg-Königstuhl State Observatory opened here in 1898.

Old University Heidelberg

Founded in 1386, Universität Heidelberg is Germany's oldest university. The most traditional university departments are centered around the Universitätsplatz in the heart of the Old Town. The Old University building, which dates back to the 18th century, can also be found here. The building houses the Rector's Office as well as the university museum, which was established in 1996. The famous historic student prison (Studentenkarzer) is located in the back of the Old University. From 1778 until 1914, students were imprisoned here for minor misbehaviors, which were kind of fashionable among otherwise honorable gentlemen.

Philosophenweg

Located to the north of the Old Bridge, the zigzagging Schlangenweg, or Snake Path, leads visitors up to the Philosophenweg, a picturesque path that stretches along the side of All Saints' Mountain. The Philosophers' Way is named after the great thinkers and educators of the university town who have walked and talked here for hundreds of years. The walking trail ends at the Philosophers' Garden, a sheltered place where warm-weather plants and flowers thrive. Many find the views offered here of the river valley and of the red-topped roofs of the city reminiscent of the Tuscany region in Italy.

Heidelberg Marktplatz

Located in the center of the Altstadt, or Old Town, the Heidelberg Marktplatz has been the city's main gathering place since the Middle Ages. Accused criminals were once dragged from the town hall on one side of the market square or from the church at the other to meet their fate. Those accused of heresy were burned at the stake. Others were left chained to the still-standing Herkulesbrunnen, a Baroque fountain that features a statue of Hercules. Nowadays, visitors come to the Marktplatz to shop. Fresh flowers, fish and produce are sold here on Wednesday and Saturday mornings.

Carl Theodor Bridge

A Heidelberg landmark, the Carl Theodor Bridge was named after the Prince Elector who ordered the bridge's construction in the 1780s. Spanning the Neckar River, the pedestrian-only sandstone bridge connects the old town quarter with the hilly landscapes on the north side of the city. The twin-towered medieval bridge gate on the old-town side was once part of the town's fortifications. West of the gate, visitors often pause to have their photograph taken before the Heidelberg Bridge

Monkey. The bronze statue holds a mirror as a reminder that people are much the same wherever their travels take them.

Heidelberg Castle
Perched high on a hill overlooking the city, the picture-perfect ruins of the Heidelberg Castle are the result of many centuries of building and of destruction caused by war, fire and pillaging. The earliest fortifications were constructed in the 13th century; most of the present structures date back to the Renaissance Era. While much of the castle remains in a state of artful decay, some rooms have been fully renovated. The interior of the King's Hall has been restored to its Gothic glory and is still used today for seasonal festivals and community events.

Heidelberg Altstadt
Heidelberg's glorious old town rests in the shadow of the ruins of Schloss Heidelberg.

The Altstadt has many of the things people love about German old quarters; sociable squares with bar terraces at Kornmarkt and Marktplatz, cobblestone streets and a catalogue of historic landmarks.

These can be Gothic or Baroque churches, or monuments like the statue of Mary on Kornmarkt from 1718, a symbol of Heidelberg's complicated relationship with Catholicism.

One of the interesting features of the Altstadt is that it has a uniform Baroque appearance, a result of fires caused by a French assault in 1693 during the Nine Years' War.

The Town Hall was built in the aftermath and dates to 1701, still featuring the electoral coat of arms sculpted by Hungarian artist Heinrich Charrasky.

Schloss Heidelberg

Perched 80 metres above the Altstadt and Neckar is the former seat of Heidelberg's Prince Electors, now one of the most beautiful ruins in the world.

The castle was begun as a fortress in the 13th century, but in the 15th and 16th century was expanded into a palace fit for Heidelberg's imperial rulers.

The next 300 years weren't exactly kind to Schloss Heidelberg as the property suffered fire from thunderbolts and repeated destruction during the Thirty Years' War in the 1600s and the Nine Years' War less than 100 years later.

From then the complex was only partly reconstructed, and its ruins inspired Germany's Romantics and were depicted by Turner during two separate stays.

Visit for an audio tour of the extraordinary Renaissance ruins, and for the Pharmacy Museum, which we'll cover later.

Alte Brücke (Old Bridge)

Crossing the Neckar between the Altstadt and the Neuenheim district on the right bank, the Alte Brücke dates in its current form to 1788 during the rule of Elector Charles Theodore.

Despite being more than 200 years old, this structure is the ninth bridge to be built on this spot.

Each bridge built from the 1200s to the 1700s was wrecked by ice floes in spring, but the current one has survived because it was the first to be built entirely from stone.

The bridge is embellished with two sets of sculpture, one paying homage to Charles

Theodore and another to the Roman goddess Minerva.

These are replicas, and the originals were transferred to the Kurpfälzisches Museum for safekeeping.

On the bank of the Altstadt is a pair of towers from Heidelberg's Medieval fortifications.

Deutsches Apotheken-Museum
Across 11 rooms in Schloss Heidelberg is a museum documenting the history of pharmacies and medical science in Germany.

There are 20,000 pieces on display here, but what really captures the imagination are the seven complete pharmacy sets, the earliest dating back to the Renaissance.

The museum has what is claimed to be the world's largest collection of 18th-century earthenware, as well as valuable majolica, faience and technical glass containers and equipment from the 1600s to the 1800s.

There are also fascinating home or portable pharmacy kits, including a sensational example made mostly from silver in Augsburg in 1640. And you can learn more about the strange things that went in these pots, like bezoar stones, mandrake root and mummia (sometimes made from powdered Egyptian mummies!).

Heidelberg Tun
In the cellar of Schloss Heidelberg is a marvel that also needs its own entry.

The Heidelberg Tun is an enormous wine barrel.

It was built in 1751 during the reign of Charles Theodore and when it was completed was able to hold 221,726 litres.

Since then its capacity has shrunk by a couple of thousand litres as the wood has aged.

A container of this size required timber from130 oak trees! The Heidelberg Tun is in fact the fifth in a line of outsized wine barrels at the palace, going back to the first barrel from the 16th century that was destroyed in the Thirty Years' War.

The barrel has only been used for wine a few times in its history and was filled just three times.

This was done from the floor above via a hole in the ceiling of the cellar

Studentenkarzer
On Augustinergasse in a Baroque building at the back of the Old University is a small jail where students were temporarily locked up for minor offences.

The jail was in use from the 1770s to the dawn of the First World War, and students would end up here for any number of reasons.

For many it was because of drunken behaviour, practical jokes on the university or city authorities or even duelling, which remained a common activity right up to 1914. Students would be released to attend lectures, but were expected to return to the jail to stay out their sentence, which could last for up to a month.

The reason you have to see the Studentenkarzer is for the graffiti and pictures covering the walls of the jail by students bragging about their exploits.

Parks and Gardens

Plenty of recreational spaces are available around the city of Heidelberg, offering peaceful spots to sit and relax, trails for walking, jogging and cycling, and also playground areas for children. If you are in the mood for a stroll around some pretty gardens, then the English-style planting within the gardens at Heidelberg Castle is a good place to start.

A rather unexpected horticultural treat and always popular with those who have a love of all things oriental, the Heidelberg Bonsai Museum is quite unmissable. Plant lovers will also find that a visit to the University Botanic Gardens is a great way to pass the time. Heidelberg's most noteworthy parks and gardens are displayed here.

Philosophenweg

Address: North of the Neckar River, Heidelberg, Germany, DE

A particularly famous German pathway running alongside the Neckar River and valley, the

Philosophenweg offers a peaceful escape from the crowded streets of Heidelberg city centre, although be prepared for a fairly steep climb. Passing though vineyards, orchards and many areas of extreme natural beauty, expect to enjoy exceptional views of the Altstadt district. Nearby are a number of popular hiking trails and hills, while a neighbouring meadow is home to several summer fireworks displays and is sited right next to the Neckar River itself.

Open hours: daily - 24 hours. Admission: no charge

Fairy Tale Park

Address: Königstuhl, Heidelberg, Germany, DE

Tel: +49 06221 234 16

Located at the top of the Königstuhl hill and connected by a funicular railway, the family orientated Fairy Tale Park is suitable for children of all ages. Highlights include many themed areas and characters, an impressive playground and even some fun hobby horses.

Open hours: March to June, September and October, Monday to Friday - 10:00 to 18:00; July and August, daily - 10:00 to 19:00. Admission: charge, concessions available

Bonsai Museum

Address: Mannheimerstrasse 401, Wieblingen, Heidelberg, D-69123, Germany, DE

Tel: +49 06221 84 9110

The Heidelberg Bonsai Museum is home to around 100 specimen bonsai trees, with popular species including Japanese maples, zelkovas, beech, a ginkgo and several junipers. A number of the exhibits are planted as miniature forests, recreating nature in perfection. Many weekend events often take place throughout the year at the Bonsai Museum, including workshops and lectures.

Open hours: Monday to Friday - 10:00 to 18:00, Saturday and Sunday - 10:00 to 16:00. Admission: charge

University Botanic Gardens (Botanischer Garten der Universitat)

Address: University of Heidelberg, Im Neuenheimer Feld 340, Heidelberg, D-69120, Germany, DE

Tel: +49 06221 54 5783

The University Botanic Gardens are one of the true gems for plant lovers visiting Heidelberg and contain a rather diverse array of plant collections. Established at the end of the 16th century, the Botanic Gardens are amongst the oldest in Europe and therefore contain many impressive and mature specimens. Particularly popular are the greenhouse exhibits, which include flowering orchids, succulents, cacti, ferns, bromeliads and other exotic plants. In total, the gardens are home to more than 10,000 different plant species, many of which are well labelled.

Open hours: gardens, daily - 24 hours; greenhouses, Monday to Thursday - 09:00 to 16:00, Friday - 09:00 to 14:30, Sunday - 09:00 to 12:00, 13:00 to 16:00. Admission: no charge

Heidelberg Neighbourhoods, Locations and Districts

The historical city of Heidelberg attracts visitors with its inspiring architecture, medieval feel and friendly residents. Now a prominent research and educational centre, the city of Heidelberg spans 14 districts, each with their own character.

Divided by the River Neckar, the city spans both sides of the river to form a picturesque and romantic setting that was in fact the one-time home of the German Romantic movement.

Heidelberg's dozens of sites of literary, architectural and musical importance make this fascinating and enchanting German hub a great tourist destination. The main districts within Heidelberg are below.

Old Town (Altstadt)

Perhaps the most significant district for tourists is in the Old Town area of Heidelberg, where most visitors choose to reside amongst the winding, narrow alleyways. Set on the south bank of the River Neckar, the Old Town stretches inland, overshadowed by the Schloss (Castle). Best explored on foot, this condensed area contains most of the city's museums and a lively entertainment scene consisting of tavernas and pubs, as well as some more cosmopolitan restaurants. In addition, this primary district houses many of the city's historic meeting spots, including Market Place (Marktplatz), University Place (Universitätsplatz) and the Old Bridge (Alte Brücke).

Bergheim District

Facing Neuenheim across the river is the Bergheim district, centrally located just to the west of the Old Town. A charming combination of commercial and residential properties, visitors will find places to stay and restaurants to dine at more affordable prices than those in the nearby Old Town.

Handschuhsheim District

One of the city's northernmost districts, Handschuhsheim has a lengthy aristocratic history. Formerly the residence of the Handschuhsheim Dynasty, the imposing Tiefburg sits as a reminder to these days of glory. Teeming with visitor attractions, highlights include Handschuhsheimer

Schlösschen and St. Vitus Church, the latter of which is home to the ornate graves of some of the Handschuhsheim. This part of Heidelberg is also a hotspot for gourmands and has the advantage of being off the beaten tourist track.

Kirchheim District

Visited mostly for its Tombs of Merowinger, dating from the Stone Age, this westerly district underwent damage in Heidelberg's 17th century conflicts.

After this turbulent century, the area mushroomed with development and became part of Heidelberg proper in 1920. Modern outlets make this a good district for shopping and dining.

Neuenheim District

Residing on the north bank of the river, Neuenheim was founded by the Romans as a fishing settlement. Boasting some stunning residential sites built in the Art Nouveau style, the district became favoured among intellectuals in the 19th century and is nowadays home to many educational institutes. Resident students and researchers keep this district lively and its sports grounds full. Of interest to visitors is the Botanical Garden and Heidelberg Zoo, both top attractions in their own right.

Südstadt / Weststadt Districts

Primarily a transport hub but boasting some beautiful houses characteristic of Heildelberg, Weststadt is located to the south-west of Bergheim. The sought-after residential parts of this district compete with those of the Südstadt, which now joins Weststadt to the south. Of interest is the Gaisbergturm, an architectural landmark that was built in 1876 by the Heidelberg Lock Association.

Climb the spiral staircase to the top for spectacular views of the surrounding area.

Wieblingen District

Possibly the oldest settled area in the Neckar Valley, evidence of a mammoth and a Stone Age civilisation were found here. Wieblingen's extensive history makes it an interesting place to explore, however, like much of Heidelberg, damage caused in 17th century conflicts destroyed many of its historic buildings. Recent centuries have seen it develop as a major craft and industrial centre, with attractions such as the Bonsai Museum springing up.

Ziegelhausen District

Formerly known for its brick production, quarries and mining, this quiet city district sits on the north bank opposite Schlierbach and attracts those looking for a base from which to set off hiking in the countryside, the Neckar meadows and the lush forest known as Odenwald. Also of interest within the Ziegelhausen area of Heidelberg is the Stift Neuburg, a Benedictine cloister, and the Textile Museum Max Berk, as well as several pretty churches.

Golf Courses and Clubs

Germany's Baden-Württemberg state and Karlsruhe region offer a handful of golf courses to suit all abilities, being just a short distance from the city centre and easy to reach by car. Golf courses are particularly clustered around the nearby north-westerly city of Mannheim and include the Golfclub Mannheim Viernheim. Further golf courses close to Heidelberg can be found around Eppelheim, Viernheim and Wiesloch, all of which boast modern facilities and plenty of good views.

Particularly popular, due to its close proximity to Heidelberg, is the Rhein-Neckar Golf Freizeitanlage Eppelheim Club, which lies on the city's western outskirts and is just minutes away.

Rhein-Neckar Golf Freizeitanlage Eppelheim Club

Address: Gerhart Hauptmann Strasse 3, Eppelheim, D-69214, Germany, DE

Number of holes: 18

Direction: 5 km / 3 miles west

Par: 72

Open hours: daily - dawn to dusk

Golfclub Mannheim Viernheim 1930 E.V.

Address: Alte Mannheimer Strasse 3, Viernheim, D-68519, Germany, DE

Tel: +49 06204 / 60700

Number of holes: 18

Direction: 24 km / 15 miles north-west

Par: 72

Open hours: daily - dawn to dusk

Golf- Und Landclub Wiesloch Hohenhardter Hof 1983 E.V.
Address: Hohenhardter Hof 1, Wiesloch, D-69168,

Germany, DE

Tel: +49 06222 / 788110

Number of holes: 18

Direction: 15 km / 9 miles south

Par: 72

Open hours: daily - dawn to dusk

Landmarks and Monuments

A wealth of centuries-old buildings and similar landmarks in Heidelberg serves to give the city its medieval character, making it a visitor's dream to explore on foot. The Heidelberg Castle dominates the Old Town, standing guard over the historic centre, which is set on the banks of the River Neckar.

Cross over the picturesque Old Bridge for some great photo opportunities, historic monuments and local landmarks, as well as a peek at the helmeted Bridge Gate. Those visiting Heidelberg who are prepared to walk can experience nearby sights, such as Thingstatte, a disused amphitheatre built under Nazi supervision. Heidelberg's many landmarks are below.

Heidelberg Castle (Heidelberger Schloss)

Address: Über dem Ostlichen, Ende der Altstadt, Heidelberg, D-69117, Germany, DE

Sitting high on the plateau and dominating the Old Town, the castle is Heidelberg's most well-known landmark. Visitors can access Heidelberg Castle by taking a steep climb on foot, or alternatively they can use the mountain railway (Bergbahn) from Kornmarkt. You can take a guided tour of the buildings or go at it alone. From the castle courtyard you will see various architectural styles, evidence the various parts of the castle were built in different periods. The cellar contains the largest wooden barrel in the world, and samples of wine are available. The best views of the city can be had from Belvedere terrace. Don't forget to tour the delightful English gardens, once visited by Goethe.

Open hours: daily - 08:00 to 17:00 (castle courtyard), 24 hours (castle gardens)

Admission: no charge (castle gardens), charge (castle courtyard)

Bridge Gate (Breckentor)

Address: Altstadt, Am Neckar, Heidelberg, D-69117, Germany, DE

The picturesque medieval Bridge Gate, which leads

to the Old Bridge, is an unmissable Heidelberg sight. This well-preserved gateway is sided by two white towers with Baroque helmets, and sits on the Old Town side of the Neckar River. The West Tower was formerly used as somewhere to detain miscreant, being home to dungeons, while the East Tower contains a spiral staircase.

Open hours: daily - 24 hours

Admission: no charge

Old Bridge (Alte Brucke)

Address: Altstadt, Am Neckar, Heidelberg, D-69117, Germany, DE

The picture-worthy Old Bridge is an essential stop of on any walking tour of the Old Town. Constructed in the late 18th century and spanning the Neckar River, the Old Bridge was the first stone bridge to be constructed in this spot after a series of wooden bridges were destroyed. Visitors can read the plaque here commemorating the city's success in defending Heidelberg from invading French troops in 1798. In addition, the bridge is home to sculptures produced by an 18th century official court sculpture, Franz Konrad Linck.

Open hours: daily - 24 hours

Admission: no charge

Schwetzingen Castle (Schloss Schwetzingen)

Address: Schwetzingen, Germany, DE

Schwetzingen is situated just 12 km / 7 miles from Heidelberg and is a popular daytrip destination for its castle and gardens. More of a palace than a castle, the gardens are the main attraction, where you can peacefully stroll among peacocks and a spectacular range of plants and flowers. The architectural variation of the gardens makes them even more interesting, and there is a recently restored mosque on-site. The Marktplatz in front of the castle is popular among diners and coffee lovers, with a selection of eateries and cafés to choose from.

Open hours: daily

Admission: charge

Thingstatte

Address: Auf dem Heiligenberg, Heidelberg, D-69121, Germany, DE

Heiligenberg, about a one-hour walk from the Old Town area of Heidelberg, is home to Thingstatte, a Nazi-built open-air amphitheatre. Also accessible by car, you can explore the dilapidated theatre, which was built by forced labourers. Test the acoustics while you are here - they are really quite impressive. Adjacent to the theatre is a 9th-century monastery, which was deserted at the turn of the 16th century. There is a lovely beer garden nearby and a small guesthouse for those who are too tired, or merry, to walk back to the Old Town.

Open hours: daily - 24 hours

Admission: no charge

Palais Boisseré

Address: Hauptstrasse 235, Heidelberg, Germany, DE

Located on the eastern side of Heidelberg's Markt area, the Palais Boisseré is a particularly grand, former palace building and known for its medieval architecture. The Palais Boisseré hosts a number of temporary exhibitions each year and these events are known to have once attracted many famous German poets and writers, including the Brothers Grimm, amongst others. Standing to the north of the Karlsplatzes and dating back more than 300 years, the palace is home to a permanent collection of historic Germany paintings.

Open hours: daily - seasonal variations

Admission: charge

Ruprecht Karl University Of Heidelberg (Ruprecht-Karls-Universität Heidelberg)

Address: Grabengasse 1, Heidelberg, D-69117, Germany, DE

The oldest university in the whole of Germany, the University of Heidelberg is of great historical significance and an important landmark in its own right. Heidelberg University was originally split into four main faculties - law, medicine, philosophy and also theology, and previously was centred around the Universitätplatz. Today, the university now boasts almost 20 different faculties and is home to more than 30,000 students, with the main campus being located on the northern side of the Neckar River.

Open hours: daily

Admission: no charge

Things to Do

Events and Festivals

Local events and festivals occur frequently in Heidelberg, and visitors to Heidelberg have plenty of chances to see local residents in action.

More often accompanied by beer drinking and sausage eating than not, the festivities this city has to offer are always filled with merriment.

Among the year's highlights are the Christmas Market, magically decorated, and the Heidelberg Fall Festival, an enormous street party.

There are several magazines that are available at all newsagents offering visitors to Heidelburg listings on all forthcoming things to see and do in this vibrant city, including up-to-date information on entertainment, shopping and dining.

HEIDELBERG NATIONAL PUBLIC HOLIDAYS

- ➤ 1st January (New Year's Day)
- ➤ Late March or early April - Good Friday / Easter Sunday / Easter Monday
- ➤ 1st May (Labour Day)
- ➤ Early May - Ascension Day, 40 days after Easter
- ➤ May / June - Whit / Pentecost Sunday and Monday
- ➤ 3rd October (Day of German Unity)
- ➤ 25th December (Christmas Day)
- ➤ 26th December (Boxing Day / St. Stephen's Day)

HEIDELBERG CALENDAR OF FESTIVALS AND EVENTS 2014 / 2015

January: New Year's Day - a public holiday, celebrating the start of the new year. German's like to party on the eve preceding this day

February: Fasching - a Mardi Gras feel overtakes the city, which transforms into a party zone

Vampire Ball at Heidelberg Castle - if you are in Heidelberg in February, try to attend this fancy affair within one of the city's premier attractions. However, be prepared to dress up

March: Long Night of the Museums - March sees Heidelberg's museums open late into the night, so that visitors and residents alike can enjoy a fun and educational experience after hours

Heidelberg Fruehling - held from mid-March to mid-April, this international music festival attracts both classical and contemporary musicians, with concerts held at venues across the city

April: Easter - while more Germans participate in chocolate egg hunts than attend Mass these days, this day has not lost its religious significance altogether, with Heidelberg's churches holding special services in remembrance of the crucifixion and the resurrection of Christ at this time

May: Deutsche Bank-SAP Open Golf Tournament - golf fans will not want to miss out on this major golfing tournament held in St Leon Rot

June: Schlossbeleuchtung - an event that occurs three times a year, including on the first Saturday in June, the 'castle lighting' is a big summer attraction. The fireworks event sees residents in a festive spirit and a party atmosphere take over the city. The castle appears to be in flames before the fireworks burst into action

Heidelberg Castle Festival - this annual event is held from 23rd June to 12th August and includes festivities such as musical performances. There is also a procession in celebration of the 'Student Prince' who returns to the castle

July: Schlossbeleuchtung - the second Saturday in July is also the second 'castle lighting' event of the year, when Heidelberg Castle is lit up so as to appear it is on flames. The show culminates in a 15-minute firework display which is best seen from the 'other' side of the river

August: No significant events and festivals in Heidelberg in the month of August

September: Schlossbeleuchtung - your final opportunity to see the city's 'castle lighting' is on the first Saturday in September. Just after nightfall, the castle is lit up so that it appears as though it is on fire. An impressive fireworks display follows to the delight of Heidelberg residents, who take up spots all along the river and at Philosophenweg

Heidelberg Fall Festival (Heidelberger Herbst)-29th September, probably Heidelberg's most popular festival known throughout Germany, where the city takes to the streets to party on. Expect local beer to be flowing readily and hot sausages are on hand for merry revellers

October: German Unity Day - 3rd October, this nation-wide celebration in commemoration of the Reunification of Germany. Marking the re-merging of East and West Germany, Heidelberg residents celebrate the birth of the Federal Republic of Germany

November: Christmas Market - held from 24th November to 22nd December, the Christmas Market is one of the annual highlights of Heidelberg. Open daily from late morning until around 21:00, aside from the magic atmosphere, this is a great place to do your gift shopping. Even if you do not purchase any of the unique arts and crafts for sale, make sure you sample some of the speciality foods such as the tasty German sausages and mulled wine

December: Christmas Day - celebrated on the 25th December, people in Heidelberg and throughout Germany participate in gift giving and family get-togethers on this day. The city is adorned in illuminated decorations in the month proceeding, with the Christmas Market helping residents to get into the festive spirit

Restaurants and Dining

Heidelberg has plenty of dining options available and good food can be found within a variety of eateries, ranging from brewpubs and central pavement cafes, to historic taverns and gourmet restaurants. Whilst this is an important university city with a base of more than 25,000 students, there are few cheap eats here, being outweighed by plush restaurants, targeted at tourists and offering regional specialities from all over the world.

Many of the best restaurants within Heidelberg feature an extensive selection of regional wines, which provide a great accompaniment to any meal, whatever the time of day. For those who prefer a stein of German beer when dining out, rest assured that beer will always be in plentiful supply, together with plenty of locally produced wine from the Baden region.

What to Eat

With many southern specialities and regional dishes appearing on the menus of the innumerable restaurants in Heidelberg, tourists have plenty of opportunity to sample the local fare.

The cuisine within Heidelberg tends to be dominated by dairy produce, when compared to the somewhat meatier dishes within northern Germany, although grilled bratwurst sausages and snail soup are still fairly commonplace here. When dining out at Heidelberg's German-style restaurants, look out for the following dishes:

- ➢ Bibbeleskäs - locally produced cottage cheese
- ➢ Brägele - fried slices of potato
- ➢ Flädlesuppe - tasty broth with ribbons of pancake
- ➢ Knöpfle - thick noodles
- ➢ Schupfnudeln - potato-based pasta
- ➢ Sauerkraut - sour, fermented shredded cabbage

Freshwater fish also makes up much of the local menus, while those with a more international palate will find Italian, Chinese, Thai, and Mexican restaurants in good supply, amongst others.

Where to Eat

Many of the most popular restaurants in Heidelberg can be found lining much of the Hauptstrasse, a street literally crammed with dining options of all descriptions. Restaurants along Hauptstrasse offer local dishes from many different cultures, ranging from German fare and vegetarian dishes, to French bistros and Italian-style eateries.

The opening hours of these restaurants also often vary greatly, according to demand.

The historic old city part of Heidelberg also contains plenty of fine dining and traditional Germany fare, including some of the city's best restaurants and brewhouses. Particularly notable in Heidelberg are those eateries located along both the Steingasse and the Untere Neckarstrasse, a number of which are housed in historic buildings dating back to the beginning of the 18th century. For cafes and lunchtime snacks, many of the public squares around this area Heidelberg are lined with cheap eats and outside tables, such as the Uniplatz and also the Marktplatz, off the Auf der Hauptstrasse

Shopping and Districts

Those who enjoy a day out shopping will find the city of Heidelberg an appealing place to spend their money. The many shopping streets of Heidelberg are particularly attractive and lined with charming, period shops and sympathetically restored buildings.

Home to some of the most attractive shopping precincts in Germany, many of the shops in the city stand alongside pavements cafes, bars, restaurants and bistros, providing you with plenty of opportunity to take a break, sit at an outside table and watch the other shoppers passing by.

When to Shop and Opening Hours

In recent years, the shopping hours of Heidelberg and Germany as a whole have become rather more relaxed. Many shops around the city now remain open until as late as 20:00 Monday through Saturday, although specific hours do vary, with smaller local shops often choosing to close earlier and may also take a long break at lunchtime. Most shops are not allowed to open on Sundays, although some local bakeries do open early in the morning.

Where to Shop

Amongst the best shopping in Heidelberg, the Hauptstrasse is an appealing, pedestrianised precinct and home to many high-street names and major stores. The Hauptstrasse stretches for around 1 km / 0.6 miles and will be sure to provide a particularly memorable shopping experience, with fashion boutiques, gift shops, local speciality stores and more.

Further shopping can be found along the winding side streets of Heidelberg's Old Quarter, with shops being particularly plentiful along the Untere Strasse and also around the Heiliggeistkirche church. Ranging from antiques stores and art galleries, to jewellery and clothing outlets, many affordable and quirky souvenirs are on offer in this part of the city.

The End

Lightning Source UK Ltd.
Milton Keynes UK
UKHW011345081222
413590UK00005B/796